About the Author

MICHAEL MCTAGUE has been studying poetry for many years before he started creating poetry. He completed his doctoral dissertation at the University of Iowa by comparing translations of *Beowulf*. His studies span medieval and modern literature as well as Old Norse, Latin works and Dante. Over the years, he has taught many courses in literature, writing and business. He is the author of *The Businessman in Literature: Dante to Melville*, published by The Philosophical Library.

    A New York native, his poems draw from a variety of experiences in and out of the largest city in the US. Dr. McTague has taught many college-level courses. He also studied Poetics with the Pulitzer Prize-winning American poet, James Wright.

He spends a good deal of his time working at a private equity firm in New York. In this role, he has worked with companies in energy, pharmaceuticals, medical equipment, travel services, mining, higher education and other industries to secure financing. He has written numerous articles on business and contributes to Equities.com. You can find him on his Amazon author's page. In 2020, he published *Secrets of Effective Business Plans*. He is the author of *Poems from the Top of the World* and *From the Edge of Europe to Yankee Stadium*, both published by Pegasus.

The Generals Speak
and Other Poems

Michael McTague

The Generals Speak
and Other Poems

Vanguard Press

VANGUARD PAPERBACK

© Copyright 2024
Michael McTague

The right of Michael McTague to be identified as author of this work has been asserted by him in accordance with the Copyright, Designs and Patents Act 1988.

All Rights Reserved

No reproduction, copy or transmission of this publication may be made without written permission.
No paragraph of this publication may be reproduced, copied or transmitted save with the written permission of the publisher, or in accordance with the provisions of the Copyright Act 1956 (as amended).

Any person who commits any unauthorised act in relation to this publication may be liable to criminal prosecution and civil claims for damages.

A CIP catalogue record for this title is available from the British Library.

ISBN 978 1 80016 883 1

*Vanguard Press is an imprint of
Pegasus Elliot Mackenzie Publishers Ltd.*
www.pegasuspublishers.com

First Published in 2024

**Vanguard Press
Sheraton House Castle Park
Cambridge England**

Printed & Bound in Great Britain

Contents

Originale	9
The Generals Speak	11
Malthus Strikes Again	13
De Senectute	15
A Night for Ivy	18
At the Last Supper	20
What Goes First	23
Get Rich Quick	25
That Wood	27
You're Just a *North* American	29
Clueless President	32
What Will Today Bring?	34
Schizophrenic Nightmare	36
Over Her Head	38

Originale

"Originale! Originale!" the street hawker bellows
Short lad wearing a Schwarzenegger shirt
And a New York Yankees hat. Selling artworks
At the bottom of the Spanish Steps by the Fountain of the
    Boat.

Italian masters mixed with movie stars.
No original works of art. All prints.
In this crazy world, can anyone be trusted,
Where truth conceals itself in a fake masquerade?

No Grecian urn for sale from any who peddle.
Not even a modified Etruscan replica for the scholarly.
Surely the poetic history casts some noticeable spell
Over the fakers who control these *sampietrini*.

None of these tourists knows that Keats and Shelley
Lived just below the Trinità dei Monti.
Or how much Byron loved this ancient city.
A beautiful world is at our feet as vulnerable as our own
    clay.

In neighborhood of a fountain, without the noise
Soft showering in my ears. Only the shrieks
Sans merci of these infernal bag sellers.
Will the noise never end? I have such fears.

The Generals Speak

Maps spread out on floors and tables everywhere.
"You can attack here, but you can't bomb there."
"Don't be stupid. That is definitely a museum!"
"That's a monastery on top of that mountain."
"Hell no! Dates from the time of Leonardo and
 Michelangelo."
"Yes. I guess they spoke Latin that long ago."
Italy's nothing but a GD museum.

Keep marching. The devils have no heart.

Stuck here without support, no naval bombardment.
Across the Pacific, planes unable to strike from our carriers.
Planners in Washington trying to sketch
How to end this awful Death March.
No food or water. We have surrendered our weapons
Here we walk, prodded with bayonets.
We're all together on this. *I shall return.*

Must sleep on the cold mountain
With rain and ice in my face.
Higher and colder every foot.
Amazing, the men and the elephants
Can stand the long, grueling pace.
The enemy may be fresh when we surprise them.
Must keep everyone fed and warm.
I will either find a way or make one.

We are poorly armed workmen and farmers.
Tired of our miserable peasant lives.
Something new is surely coming.
Must plod onward, never collapsing
Under the overwhelming sting
Of their never-ending gunfire.
The Long March has proclaimed their utter failure
to encircle, pursue, obstruct and intercept us.

Malthus Strikes Again

Consider the peculiar British perspective on land
Must have new earth at all costs even if a war must be won.
Head for Australia if you don't like cloudy London,
Or Canada. Don't forget picturesque New Zealand.

Stay away from those independent Americans.
They want the empire to feature a setting sun.
Land is good. Power is even more satisfying,
Despite the warning of Lord Acton.

Rich, black soil may fill the distant steppes.
Can't go East. You'll wind up in Turkey or Siberia.
Where does that leave Thomas Malthus?
Reduces him to just another economic theory.

Malthus was right! There's not enough farmland.
It's much worse all across the modern European Union
Agriculture only holds its own in Portugal and Spain.
Everyone searching for higher crop production.

Banks and investing from Finland to Netherlands
All across this hungry, overcrowded continent

Banking, machine making, auto manufacturing,
Wealth creation, pill production, credit card processing.

Up and down the old continent the money trickles
Investors looking for the big payday
Hedge funds ramp up stores of money
While IPOs grab massive bundles of capital.

The future no longer poses a real military threat.
All around, bountiful harvests, healthy, fatted animals.
While the farmer gets little respect.
Lost in a world of manufacturing and services.

Long before government involvement and balance of payments
Prior to Keynes and Leontiev using their heads
Centuries ahead of the Green Revolution and plant hybrids
Men and animals fretted about our daily bread.

De Senectute

Sorry, Yeats, Cicero had it right. Old men's capabilities stun us.
New ideas are so often brought forth by old politicians.
At least in the United States. Where Biden rules
He and predecessor Trump stand atop the age list of starting Presidents.

Why indeed does youth so often turn to the elderly for insight?
Only the aged possess the knowledge gained from a life well spent
Drawing from the memory of so many worthy endeavors --
Spanning education, family, military, entire careers.

More important than their experience on the bench
Youth rules in every Supreme Court Justice search.
The wisdom of elderly judges comes after their time as youthful nominees.
Angry revolutionaries seek to latch onto future elders.

Living past 100 is no great hurrah.

Put together, centenarians would fill Atlanta,
Wyoming or Kansas City. Also Omaha.
Wonder what the elderly Oracle would say.

The Senate is no place for young men.
Now the comfortable home of so many octogenarians
Who keep getting returned to Washington
If they don't lose elections to septuagenarians.

Every place you look, old age overwhelms us.
Queen Elizabeth outdid all other monarchs.
Cultures that worship youth always
Find themselves with the oldest leaders.

Benedict XVI was the oldest of his noble class
Living longer than all fourteen Clements.
Pope Leo XIII amazed the Cardinals but he
Only made it to the age of ninety-three.

Old actors snatch awards; youngsters applaud and leap.
Ask Anthony Hopkins, Daniel Day-Lewis
Or three-time winner Meryl Streep.
Who learned their craft over many decades.

Yūichirō Miura at 80 outdoes Norgay and Hillary
Tom Brady plays beyond the greats of yesterday.
Klitschko tops Jersey Joe for age durability
As well as Dempsey, Willard and Ali.

Vietnam, cancer or a STEMI heart attack
Don't present much of a setback
A team of top-notch surgeons
Will rapidly insert a stent, a fountain of youth, and extend your life for many years.

A Night for Ivy

The dais finally fully filled.
The chicken dinner at last served.
The chairman and the captain read over their notes.
They will soon address the ravenous guests.

Parents hold a finger to their mouths
Quieting the excited youngsters.
Photographers toy with their cameras,
Checking the flash. Ready for a tight focus.

Waiters hurry with overloaded trays.
Smoke rises under the No Smoking signs.
Clergy edge a little closer to say grace
A politician ready to advocate for independence.

Winners and losers of "Footballers of the Year"
Gathered for the trophies they worked so hard for.
Coaches fidget with their ties at the first few tables.
Managers ready to take hold of the prized cups

Scraps of conversation rise.
"When you put the shoe into him, John."

"McGoldrick. Ahha, there was the man!"
"A good man on his hind legs."

"He had a secret plan to withdraw." "No other option."
"He wasn't really guilty. He meant no harm."
"I'd have done the same if I were him."
"Ahh, no! Who's going to cast the first stone?"

"Ivy for your lapel, Father Shea?"
 "Partition must go. Come what may."
"They should give back the missing six."
 Wide wrists raising pints of Guinness.

Football is the subject; rebellion the inspiration.
Informers suspected, wearing phony smiles
Everywhere can be found defenders of the informed upon.
"Up the rebels!" shouted from the Leitrim tables.

One might see the same heavy eyebrows and tattered sleeves.
Rough hands, boots with wooden cleats.
Word for word, speakers make the same remarks.
And so it goes for well over one hundred years.

At the Last Supper

The table is set. "Give us… our daily bread".
The loaves passed in a basket from hand to hand.
The wine has already gone all the way around.
Simon Peter smiles. Thaddeus bows his head.

Jesus surveys the scene as he did on the Mount.
Food brings all together. Everyone appears content.
An attendant pours cool water from a large jar.
Judas laughs, looks around and kisses the air.

The plates are empty but soon all will eat.
This is no *simple* wine-changing event.
Most will stand by him as the trying times roll out.
One at least will reveal himself as a rat.

Every large group contains at least one spoiler.
Can the turncoat be noticed from his eyes?
What motivates him or any betrayer?
Money? Approval? Jealousy? So many possibilities.

Even in this carefully chosen band of brothers
Not just one assembled by blood line
Like Cain and Abel, born of the same mother

The force of the moment stimulates the stool pigeon.

A grudge, a private slight, a public fight
A personal brawl supplies the weight
It takes to break any long-standing bond,
Making an enemy of your closest friend.

Factions are easy to form. They appear set in stone
But last only for a time until the damage is done.
So many will rise, and for a short time burn hot
Then collapse as the centuries run past.

Long before the signing of the US Constitution
People knew about human division.
Unity seems to last, but so easily flames out.
When times turn bad, conviction will evaporate.

Let bad times roll in and the unity of violence brings many
    together
Action follows quickly. So it was in those long-past times,
In our own troubled era that finds brother against brother,
The destructive nature of evil frequently reappears.

So it is also the way of heaven considering the fallen
    angels.
One rebel, armed with evil desire and strong words,
Drawing upon human suffering, promising to deliver the
    basics
But bringing about barren emptiness.

A way with words, mixed with a scattering of activity
Feed only a few. Deliver very little.
While the moral are busy in a frenzy.
Taking on more than they can handle.

But this group is the core, imperfect in so many ways
Shortly to be found arguing about their undying loyalty
These will soon change the world by penetrating
Deep into the hearts of all who will listen.

What they eat this day means little – merely providing
A setting for a group of friends, gathering, dining together
Not fully aware of their role as changemakers
Who will commence after the fury of the passion.

The long marches, the stormy sea voyages,
The battles fought and finally won.
Peter will look back after many decades.
As will Philip and Andrew, James and John.

Unleavened bread, figs, dried pomegranates, beans,
Will not make a mark on believers.
Few concern themselves with what was eaten.
And so Leonardo shows many empty dishes.

Hands in motion. Everyone conversing.
Not a single individual eating.
It's all about the great anticipation
Of the troubling days and the task's completion.

What Goes First

Have you ever watched a loved one slip away
Into something less than what they were in their prime
When we first got to know them?
Think back: Which essential faculty is first to evaporate?

After losing a sense of guilt, the slippage accelerates
They hurt someone and show no feeling of dread
Say the wrong thing and stand blank-faced
While old friends rail about the lack of sentiment.

Everyone gets angry, sometimes for good reason
People slip and utter a predictable litany of bad words
A few droop morally and commit unthinkable sins
Good people feel remorse quickly before their rash
    behavior sinks in.

We dive into a pool of evil when we lose the sense of guilt
Almost no one thinks about digging themselves out.
Laws, police, courts may pin us down, hold us back.
In a pointless effort to get us back on track.

Within the individual human heart

Lies the ultimate arbiter of what is right.
It's so easy to veer off
And never get back to our true self.

Get Rich Quick

Hate to wait? You have plenty of company.
Buying and holding saps the excitement
Of investing and totaling one's property
In the counting house all through the night.

Don't be a working stiff and wait 'til you're ancient.
Take a chance. Buy gold right away.
Build up that thick wallet
Retire to the beach in Florida early.

Must be a system, a trick. Just like crossword puzzles
Or Monopoly or poker. Carefully watch the odds.
Predict market upticks. Stay away from slumps.
The game is to amass wealth, not spend it.

Think of the grieving widow at the reading
Of the will, too old to enjoy a real fling.
The grandchildren still too young
To seize the day and do their thing.

Wait for dividends? Invest in bonds?
Too slow! People want a speedy result

Even though they are not ready to stop their labors.
Life is short. Make money. Have dessert first.

Will gold leap ahead in this economy?
Must I speed up by tapping into a hedge fund
To beat the Dow, NASDAQ and S&P?
And watch my personal wealth shoot upward?

I could get by with the funds I possess
But if only I could turn the tables
To make those droopy penny stocks
Leapfrog the slow-moving blue chips.

That Wood

Dying on a cross, made from wood.
Just a long piece of lumber
Known to carpenters and to builders.
The source of paper to writers.

Acacia possibly *formed* the Ark.
In the Book of Numbers, Moses
Crafted a snake on a wooden stick.
In the desert, to heal the Israelites.

The Romans mounted Jesus on a cross.

Possibly pine. Cedar and cypress have their advocates.
Ennobling all forests of ancient and modern times.
Every city park and leafy street serves to remind us.

Its aroma and power to cleanse characterizes pine.
Acacia is well-known for resisting decay.
Cedar, valued for its hardness, a symbol of eternity.
Cypress, a mighty tree connoting our need to mourn.

Sturdy and long-lived, all trees
Catalogue everything that happens.
Standing by as people do their deeds
Often outliving their planters.

Thoreau delved into a forest's power
To breathe life into the human heart.
There is much that Wordsworth gleaned
From those little lines of sportive wood.

The true cross was discovered after Helena's
Furious search many centuries hence.
Imagine the discoverers touching a nail
Seeing the blood, seeking a miracle

More common than gold or diamonds.
Found on all but one continent,
Trees embody our greatest aspirations
Both on and beyond our planet.

You're Just a *North* American

Events in Latin America matter.
We all need to worry about Chile's copper,
And the miners who dig in the tunnels,
Argentina's beef and Niagara-topping Iguazu Falls

People from the United States aren't the only Americans.
They are merely one group, *North* Americans
Holding no claim on the Carabobo or Galapagos
Or the Tupi or the breathtaking Andes.

Not to mention Panama's golden frogs.
Don't tell me about the Alamo.
You aren't honest-to-goodness Texans.

Looking north and east but never south toward Mexico.

Hardly anyone above the Dry Tortugas
Speaks a single word of Portuguese.
No one is passionate about rum
Or appreciates life in Ipanema.

Your Florida neighbors may be evil tyrants
Who absconded with the government's assets.
Living comfortably in Naples or Miami
Where Bolivar is only a neighbor of Port St. Lucie.

People live by the peso, real and sol south of San Antonio
Until they default and start all over again.
Borrowing from a New York bank or from Washington
While the dollar explodes on the mercado negro.

Just because you conquered yellow fever,
Built the post-Delesseps Canal,
Does that mean you are something special,
Deserving some particular honor?

The Conquistadors knew that size matters.
Look at their faith, their massive churches.
Try Our Lady of Aparecida or the bishop's seat in Rio
Lima's Cathedral reflects the greatness of El Pulpo.

Ferdinand and Isabella sought the quicker route to the Indies

They knew the world was round and formed that bond with
 Columbus.
They were no dreamers. Lima and Mexico City may no
 longer be the hot spots.
That's because history plays so many cruel tricks.

Visit, look around. Climb the mountains.
Watch us live. Walk across the Atacama Desert.
Judge us by getting to know all about us
Not simply by our noisy expatriates.

Clueless President

Must give another speech -- to the Student Music Society
Have to hand out awards. Dvorak and Smetana
Evaluated by our own Professor Swoboda
Ma Vlast or bust and the New World Symphony.

Stay serious. Dvorak is moving up stream fast
Getting up there with Beethoven and Mozart
Must work that into my speech for effect.
The music faculty will really like that.

When I read Henry James, I wondered what Maisie knew.
If I had only specialized in Ernest Hemingway
Would I be lecturing on *Death in the Afternoon*?
Reminds me. Due for a meeting with the college attorney.

I really felt good dismissing the two rowdy transfer students.
Guilty of inappropriate language and public drunkenness.
At college every word, every private action, has become off limits
Even without the presence of anger, malice or wickedness.

Then there's football, that non-stop college nemesis.
Is this really the core of a modern campus?
Better not let that question ever come from my lips.
Would offend the people really in charge -- parents and
 donors.

The Board wants a report next meeting on our finances.
Only two weeks from now. Watch the tension explode
Phone calls, text messages, late nights for the accountants.
This time for sure, the numbers must show a measurable
 upgrade.

What Will Today Bring?

What came my way yesterday? Sometimes I cannot remember
I'm getting like so many others. Just want to survive.
Why work? Let Washington flood my mailbox with checks
I don't need a position. Just enough to keep myself alive.
Of course, a few extra potatoes and a case of liquor helps.

Saul Bellow was on target: "Seize the Day."
Show a serene surface. Agree, smile, go with the flow.
Keep your anxiety to yourself. Don't stand up for principles.
Dress well. Never show your true feelings.
Give in to the rules of the game and to troublemakers.

Hope the students or administrators don't discover.
Be on time – a good policy to ward off busybodies
Simply dip into the memory bank for pregnant quotations
Mix in a little purple prose. Ask students to take notes.
Know ahead the play and line especially with Shakespeare.

This always works: "Neither a borrower nor a lender…"

"In Hamlet, Shakespeare – well, he portrays
Polonius as a meddler, a fool, an intruder."
"God has given you one face, and you make yourselves another."
"Spoken by Hamlet. Ah, the play within the play! True of all of us."

"Of course in Othello, the main character's suspicions
Reflect a Freudian tendency." That scores!
"Which one? Well, that's not our subject in this class."
"Othello is tragedy. Real, classical tragedy.
Yes, Aristotle defined it. And we all should see it immediately."

Schizophrenic Nightmare

I see him. It's the devil!
Right there in that curtain
As plain as night. His eyes dark green
Looking into my tormented soul.

He knows me and I know him.
Looks like my brother. The one who's older.
Might be my brother. I won't press the matter.
He is real! Can't you see him?

Must be careful whom I talk to.
People may think I'm psycho.
After all my scholarly accomplishments.
A few even say I might be dangerous.

You're my best, my only friend, my lifeline.
If I can't convince you, I'm out of it.
The white coats have no compassion.
Just follow procedure. Listen for only a minute.

The nurse smiles wanly. Calls for backup.
Grab, jostle, poke. Always subdue.

No one asks. They squeeze, inject, pump.
I fall into a stupor for a day or two.

Thorazine and Mellaril burn my skin.
Dope me out. Make me swoon.
I thirst. I am in serious pain.
No one notices. No one cares to intervene.

One slip and your friends doubt you.
I'm just asking for a fair hearing.
Look at the trouble I'm having
Trying to convince my best friend: you.

Sometimes I'm stuck in a straitjacket
Can't move. Can't talk. Can't eat.
Me! Used to enjoy risotto. Imagine!
Occasionally even Beef Wellington.

Protein is the thing for the brain. No cannolis.
These fools! I'm schizophrenic, not diabetic.
Now, it's white bread and orange juice
Ah! What a boring way to exist.

Must dig myself out from this slough of despond
That crushes my spirit, rattles my equilibrium,
And threatens daily to end my very life span.
Don't worry. I'll hang on. Just to spite them.

Over Her Head

Sara eats a Slim Fast bar pondering financial problems
What to do! The college needs a new dorm and classrooms
No cash for such a project. Must borrow massive funds.
Debt is dangerous and Oh! the approval process!

Why can't we be like Cuba or the Netherlands?
Where everything is free, paid for by taxes.
Imagine us defaulting. We're not one of the BRICS.
Wish we were Venezuela with its untapped oil pools.

It's my job to recommend this burdensome borrowing
Why does it fall to me to be the spokesperson?
Isn't it enough to sit on top of this collegial gang
And order others around to vote for this undertaking?

How did we get onto Heightened Cash Monitoring?
Doesn't anybody ever tell me the bottom line?
Debt structure… so far from Robert Frost
Hemingway, Hawthorne or Dashiell Hammett

Everyone complains about things that are unimportant
Food service, white boards, library hours

Whispering and writing poison pen letters
More conspirators here than Macbeth or Hamlet.

So, we missed a major financial deadline.
Is that really such a gigantic circumstance?
We're all about *access* to higher education.
Why does everyone fret over paying the price.

What do these rich Board members expect from this band
    of scholars?
Austerity? Silly euro zone term for the uneducated!
Isn't it enough to sign, seal and stamp their diplomas?
And declare that like us our graduates are bona fide?

Printed in the USA
CPSIA information can be obtained
at www.ICGtesting.com
LVHW052342270824
789406LV00021B/597